Albatross

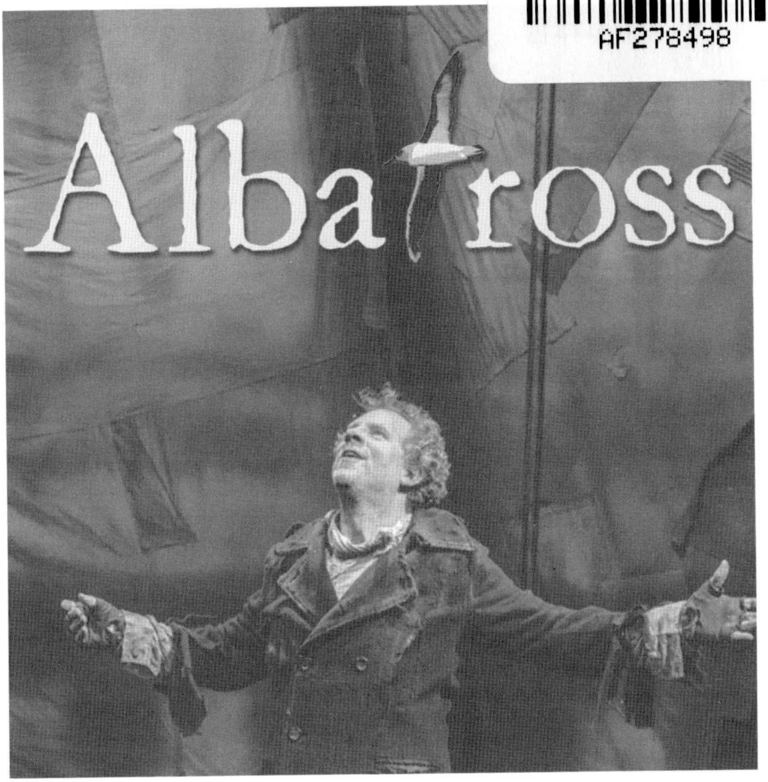

by
Matthew Spangler and Benjamin Evett

*Inspired by "The Rime of the Ancient Mariner" by
Samuel Taylor Coleridge*

STEELE SPRING
STAGE RIGHTS

www.stagerights.com

ALBATROSS

For all stage performance inquiries, please contact:

Steele Spring Stage Rights
3845 Cazador Street
Los Angeles, CA 90065
(323) 739-0413
www.stagerights.com

PRODUCTION CREDITS

First Production at the Jackie Liebergott Black Box Theatre, Boston, February 13, 2015.

Written by ....Matthew Spangler & Benjamin Evett

Performed by.. Benjamin Evett

Directed by .... Rick Lombardo

Set Design by.................................... Cristina Todesco

Costume Design by........................Frances McSherry

Lighting Design by.....................Franklin Meissner, Jr.

Projection Design by ....Aroline Herzig

Sound Design by.................................. Rick Lombardo

Props Design by....................................... Joe Stallone

Stage Managed by .... Leslie Sears

Produced by .... Mike Seiden & The Poets' Theatre

Albatross had a public reading at Arizona Theatre Company's "Café Bohemia" in April 2014.

CHARACTER DESCRIPTION

MARINER: 18th Century British sailor and navigator. Rough, uncouth, and poetic. He also voices other characters in the play.

SETTING

Bristol, England, 1720. Also a privateer ship on the high seas of the Atlantic, Antarctic, and Pacific Oceans.

PROP LIST

An iPhone
A rope
Anything else you feel you need to tell the story

AUTHORS' NOTE

The most important thing to remember is that the play is happening HERE, and it's happening NOW. The audience has come to your empty theatre, and though they believe they came of their own accord, they have actually been summoned by the Spirits because *they need to hear the story.* The Mariner appears and the Spirits help bring his story to life. In the original production, directed by Rick Lombardo, the Mariner entered with a battered, old trunk. He pulled makeshift sails out of it, which he rigged from ropes hanging from the flies. As the story began, images were projected on the sails that evoked the places and events of the story— a gloomy shack, swelling seas, the blaze of cannons. These images were underscored by an elaborate soundscape that pulled the audience into the world created by the Mariner's words. But this is only *one way* to approach the production. Make it simple, make it elaborate, whatever works for your particular circumstance. Just make it IMMEDIATE.

Finally, our Mariner is a salty dog. He peppers his language with obscenity. But he's a decent fellow at heart. If you feel your audience would absorb his story more readily if he didn't swear so much, you have our permission to clean up his language.

SCENE 1

There is no set to speak of. It seems as though another play has recently been performed, and that the company is midway through the strike: a ghost light in the center, lighting instruments lined up on the floor, ropes hanging from the ceiling, road boxes, a ladder placed to one side.

The MARINER appears. He stares at the audience.

Suddenly, he becomes gripped by an intense pain. He leans over in agony. He looks up at something, then turns to the audience.

He looks at us, not sure what to do or what to say. Then he starts telling a joke in Italian (or any language likely to be unfamiliar to the audience).

MARINER: Non sono pronto gia! Allora, iniziamo con uno scherzo: Un giorno un marinaio che ha fatto naufragio su un isola deserta vede un barile galleggiante verso la spiaggia. Diventa sempre più vicino e vede c'è una donna nuda in canna. La donna più bella che abbia mai visto. Con grandi tette. Ella striscia fuori dalla canna e cammina seducente fino al marinaio. Si sussurra in un orecchio, "Penso di avere qualcosa che si desidera." Il marinaio corre verso le onde gridando "Dimmi c'è birra in quel barile!!"

The MARINER laughs hard. After a moment, he realizes we are not laughing. He stops. Looks at us.

Capito? Vwee gavareete pa Russki?

(beat)

Ni shuo Zhongwen ma?

(beat)

An bhfuil Gaeilge agaibh?

Realizes we don't speak any of these languages. Reaches into the inside pocket of his overcoat and takes out an iPhone. Taps on it.

Un moment, sil'vous plait.

He studies the phone, then looks up in amazement. He speaks in a think dialect that is a cross between Irish and Cornish. He names the town where the play is taking place.

_____??? [wherever the play takes place]

(to the spirits)

I thought you were sending me to *Portofino*, by the sea. Instead its fuckin'
_____.

> *The MARINER makes a derogatory joke about the locale. Be mean, but not too mean.*

MARINER (CONT'D): Well, at least you speak *English*... Me bloody native tongue, so that's something.

> *(about the phone)*

An' turn these fuckers off...

> *The MARINER moves the ghost light out of the way and says the follow as he prepares the stage.*

Told this story so many times so many people so many places 'round the world, here an' there, there an' here, can't keep track... Happens all the time. My age, you get a little confused.

I'm 332 years old!

> *(referring to his good looks...)*

What do you think? Look pretty good, huh? Well preserved, as the saying goes.

> *(looks up)*

Thanks to them. The spirits. Always watching... the fuckers. Own me, drive me... sustain me.

Three centuries been telling this story. Can't die, can't sleep. Wish I could!

But the *spirits* won't let that happen. Because of what I... did.

> *(to the spirits)*

I will, I will, I'll get to it!

The spirits want me to get on with it... the story.

Always pushing, pushing us together. You an' me. What, you think you came here of your own accord? No, spirits make it happen. Everyone who hears my story *needs* to hear my story.

Like the time I met this British fella, a poet, long, long time ago. An' I feel the agony risin' up an' I grab him an' I say:

There was a ship!

An' I tell him my story. An' what does he do? Turns it into a Goddamn poem! Rhymes and everything!

It is an ancient Mariner,
An' he stoppeth one of three.
By thy long grey beard an' glittering eye,
Now wherefore stopp'st thou me?

Ancient! I wasn't *ancient*. Yet. Christ.

MARINER (CONT'D): But the thing is he doesn't get it right. Leaves things out, tells other things wrong, an' the whole story's way too fuckin' sweet, leaves all the dirt out... an' all the fuckin'... swearin'.

An' the biggest thing he leaves out is everything that happened *before,* before the bird, an'... an' the boy.

An' why I did it. Oh, yeah, because you need to know the why don't ya? In your Post-Modern, Post-Truth, Post-War, Post-Freudian, Post-Punk, Post-Deconstructionist, Post-Fucking-Post-Cereal way of life, you're always wondering why. Why? Why? Why? Why? Why?!!!! Who cares why?

> *The MARINER has finished preparing the stage. He doesn't want to go on. He sighs.*

I hate this part. Beginning. So let's not. How 'bout an old mariner's joke instead. Goes like this:

> *(the same joke the MARINER told at the start)*

One day a mariner who's been shipwrecked on a deserted island sees a barrel floating toward the beach. It gets closer an' he sees there's a naked woman in the barrel. Most beautiful woman he's ever seen. The barrel washes up on shore an' she crawls out. Walks seductively up to the mariner... whispers in his ear: "I think I have something you want." Mariner runs toward the waves shouting: "Don't tell me there's beer in that barrel!"

> *(laughs hard)*

Love that fuckin' joke!

> *He continues to laugh, then his laughter tapers off, realizing we are not laughing as much as he is.*

It's better in Italian.

> *(beat)*

The story. Okay, here we go.

Bristol, England... 1720...

The ship was cheered, the harbor cleared,
An' merrily did we drop
Below the kirk, below the hill
Below the lighthouse top.

Isn't that beautiful? So poetic. Wouldn't it be nice if that's how it actually began? Well, sorry. No such luck.

Bristol, England 1720.

SCENE 2

MARINER: I'm in the house... ruined house... *shack* more like. One stinkin' room. A crumblin' hearth over here, an' a rottin' bed of straw over there.

Bed of straw has an occupant. A boy lies in the bed. Sick. Five-year-old boy. My boy. My son. Lyin' on a bed of straw, sick.

I'm standin' over 'im. Swallow. He reaches up to me. Take his hand.

Raised the boy in me own image, see. Took 'im down the docks, on ships, showed 'im 'round, the hustle an' bustle. Always a bond, him an' me. Can't handle this shit.

He looks up at me. I see open wounds on his face. Can tell he wants me to stay.

Then *she's* there. Over me shoulder, leans into my ear: "Stay ya fucker. Don't leave me take care of 'im all by myself."

His mum. Stinkin' of gin.

I tell her: I'm just goin' down the pub, one drink, then I'll be back.

"We'll be waitin' for ya," she says. Her eyes glazed over, she's swayin' back an' forth, she can hardly stand.

I lean over, touch the boy's head. He's on fire.

I'll be back in a minute, I tell 'em.

I'd say a prayer, but I don't buy into that shite.

He looks up at me. Nods. All trust.

The mum, she goes an' sits on a stool by the hearth. Roaring fire beside her. Yeah. Middle of the fuckin' summer she's got a fire goin'. See, it's s'posed to clean the air, drive out the bad humours or some such. Bloody Enlightenment— this is what they call medicine.

"Well, hurry," she says.

An' I do. Slip out the door. Door closes behind me, hear the click.

Start headin' down the lane. See a figure standin' there... studyin' his fingernails. Oh great... *Roger*. The Jolly Roger. Oh, but you won't find his weak arse on a pirate ship. Oh, no, no. Roger the Dodger, more like. Merchant vessels only for him. Second mate's boy, nothin' more. But he's kin. Brother's son. See, when me brother ended up in jail, who knows why, mother gone, who knows where, Roger shows up at me doorstep, actin' like we're best mates or somethn', ya know, long lost pals. So I set him up... East India Trade Company.

MARINER (CONT'D): Now he's waitin' for me at the end of the lane.

Walk up.

"All right?" he asks.

Yeah, all right, I say.

"An' the boy. How is he? "

Shittin' his insides out. Lesions all over his face. Nothin' but pain. Otherwise he's fine.

"What's he got?"

Doan know.

"Is he gonna be alright?"

Doan know.

"How old is he now?"

Fuckin' questions. Five, I tell 'im.

"Five?"

Five. That's right.

"That's young. That's a young age to depart this world."

Well, he's not fuckin' gone yet now is he! He'll recover. Like all dem other kids.

"What other kids?"

All dem other kids, what were sick an' recovered!

"Right... An' the mum? She alright?"

Roger, he's a nice guy in a mean world. A bleeding heart.

Fuck her, I tell him. Can't stan' the sight of her. But *him*? Little part of me he is. I'm gonna miss him if he goes. Which he won't! *Which he fuckin' won't!*

"Alright, alright, take it easy. Getcha a pint?"

Yeah, a pint. That's more like it.

MARINER (CONT'D): Now, Roger's always broke— where he got the money for two pints, I don't know— but never turn down an offer a' drink.

An' down the lane we go.

Bristol. 1720. Second city of the Empire, second only to London, but really a shithole. Step over dead animals in the streets. Head down the hills to the docks.

Stench of death replaced by the smell of fish an' tar. The docks.

Hundreds of ships: frigates, brigs, shallops, schooners, snows, cats, hags, an' flys. Piled high with the spoils of empire: sugar, cinnamon, copper, tea. Coal outbound for the Ivory Coast, tobacco inbound from the West Indies, the middle passage dark-skinned human cargo. Loadin' 'an unloadin'. Men runnin' here an' there, tryin' to finish their work at the end of the day. Shouts, yells— "Hey, over here! *Over here, boys!* The pully! Hook it up! Pull it down!"

A fight, two men, then a mob.

Outta my way! Knock, slam, push past, down an alley betwixt the Custom House an' a warehouse.

An' then... damn... Hermit followin' us. Stinky ol' man. Smell him before you see him.

See, Hermit's well known 'round town. Makes up these crazy hymns an' then he walks the streets singin' to mariners that, as he puts it, "come from a far country."

I'm always tellin' him, I come from *here*, not some "far country." I come from *this* pisspot of a goddamn country! Got it?

Though, truth to tell, I come from nowhere. Me mother was Irish an' me father Cornish. An' me? Well, I was born somewhere between the Bristol Channel an' the Irish Sea.

Anyway,' Hermit, he's right in me face, reachin' his arms out, like, to touch me...

Get your hands off me, ol' man!

But he keeps grabbin' at me, an' then he goes into his singin', which is more like moanin'...

"Oh, thou wilt do a hellish thing.

An' it'll work 'em woe... "

Whatever the fuck that means. All I know is he won't get the fuck out of me fuckin' face!

MARINER (CONT'D): So I grab him 'round the neck, I kick his legs out from under him, an' I put him on the ground. Gently. But so he knows who's boss.

An' then, right in his face, Sing your hymns to somebody else!

Roger standing there, "Bad day, huh? You need a drink." An' he's right, I do need a drink.

Leave Hermit lying in the muck, callin' after me, "No wait!"... daft old codger.

An' on we go, 'till we enter the dark enclosure of the Drunken Duck.

Ah... the sweet smell of beer.

Know the barman. Nod. Two pints. Roger buyin'. Sit in the corner. Don't talk.

Boy's face risin' up. I push it down. Finish me pint.

Time to go back, back to the shack.

Roger says, "One more for the road."

Cheers, Roger.

Now, I'm drinkin' my pint when the Crimp walks in. See, Crimp walks with a limp ever since a barrel comin' off a ship rolled up his leg, almost snapped it in two. Now he's Crimp with a Limp.

Crimp sees us sitting there, hobbles over. Says to me...

"Hire ya for a job?"

That's what the Crimp does, see. He patrols the pubs an' docks, looking for men to go on ships.

But I say, No, more jobs, Crimp. Family man now.

"Kid's dyin'," Roger adds, like he fuckin' needs to say it.

"Lots 'a kids dyin'," Crimp says. "So what'd ya say, need a navigator. An old salt like you, best they're gonna get."

Says it 'cuz it's true. I'm the best navigator *anybody's* gonna get. One of the few who know the inlets an' outlets of that gold mine to the south, what you lot call South America.

But still, I say, No job for me, Crimp.

"It's Black Dog," Crimp says. "Black Dog's ship."

Jesus Christ, fuckin' Black Dog. One of the meanest an' richest fuckers ever to sail the high seas. Teeth like a canine, hence the name. Bite from him, like a bite from a wolf. Sometimes privateer, sometimes pirate, distinction rarely clear.

MARINER (CONT'D): Story goes, Black Dog gets picked up by the Spanish one time. Tie 'im to a chair, chains 'round his arms an' legs, start lashin' him for being a Protestant. Which is funny 'cuz Black Dog's not a Protestant nor a Catholic neither. No, if he could, he'd rip God's head off, piss down his neck an' hang him on the wall!

He waits for a laugh. It doesn't come, probably.

Anyway. They start workin' on his fingers. Put his little finger in this device between two screws. Torture man leans in. Gets ready to crush his fingers uno a uno, when Black Dog's head shoots forward, mouth agape, teeth comin' down on the man's nose, bites down, bites down hard, bites the nose clean off. Whole thing gone.

   (laughs)

Torture man screamin' now, blood pourin' out of a hole in his face. Forgets all 'bout his erstwhile occupation, crushin' fingers.

But Black Dog's not done. No... nose in his mouth see, so he chews it, an' then swallows it, an' then vomits it right back up. Bits of nose lying in a pool of blood 'an puke.

   (laughs, enjoying the story)

Too much? They let Black Dog go after that. Glad to be rid of him.

Even the Spanish Inquisition were no match for Black Dog!

Oh yeah, an' then this other time—

   The spirits wrack him with pain. He shouts up at them:

I know... I know... I know! Back to the story! Back to the story!

So, where was I? Oh, yes, Crimp. Crimp says, "What'd you say, navigator? Double share for you. Untold riches await."

But I say, no! Not workin' for that crazy loon.

Then Crimp gets right in my face, leans in.

Says, "Ah, come on. Need the best. Headin' out for parts unknown."

See his crooked teeth, smell his rotten breath.

I stand up, table moves back, screech on the floor, an' I make to smash the pint glass on his fuckin' head if he doesn't fuckin' shut the fuck up! The day I've had!

"Alright, alright!" he says.

Crimp out the door, against which glass explodes, the pint glass I threw at his fuckin' head.

Fuckin' shite!

MARINER (CONT'D) *(looks up at the spirits)*: What's that? Yeah, yeah, ok, yeah...

> *(back to us)*

Spirits think I'm swearin' too much. You know, that I'll put you off or something.

> *The MARINER makes a joke about the local people— how they're too delicate or intellectual or snowflakes, or something.*

Listen, I'm a sailor, okay? As in "Swears like a..." Right? So we understand each other.

All right. Where was I...

So I nod to the barman. Another pint. Roger buyin' again. So I have another. I mean another *after* the other.

Night comin' on. Ale house crowded now. Push me way to the bar. Drink a few more, sing a song, have another.

An' then home. Start heading for the door.

All of a sudden, the Crimp standin' there. *Again!*

Nervy blighter! I told ya, No job Crimp!

"No no no, how 'bout a pint?" he says. "Peace offering."

I don't trust Crimp, but, you know... So pretty soon I'm drinkin' it down.

I'm tellin' a story 'bout a woman, well endowed in everyway imaginable...

Story getting juicy.

When all of a sudden the bar goes all blurry, dark at the edges, an' I'm lookin' out from the bottom of a barrel! Darkness closin' in, cotton in my ears... No, wait, wait, hold on!... An' then...

> *Makes an exhale sound, claps his hands.*

An' that's it. I'm done...

SCENE 3

MARNIER: The ship was cheered, the harbor cleared,
An' merrily did we drop
Below the kirk, below the hill,
Below the lighthouse top.

A penny under the mast, an' out into the channel.

An' *that's* where I wake up. In the stuffy, bilgy, dark. Creaks, moans, an' groans.

Fuck. I'm on a ship.

Involuntary conscription. Goddamn Crimp! Slipped opium in me cup an' sold me on! Shanghaied! Abducted! Purloined! Fucked over!

I stagger up on deck an' see the spires of Bristol miles upriver.

Drag myself to the rail. Now, sailors are shitty swimmers. Point of pride. Most'll sink faster than a corpse loaded with cannon-shot. Myself included. But I think 'bout my boy. Have to do it. Foot up on the rail. Stand. Steady... Get ready for the plunge.

An' then I hear...
>   (as Black Dog)

"There's my navigator!"

Turn, see him grinnin' at me like a rabid pug. Black Dog. A crowd of mean lookin' men standin' 'round him, sniggerin'.

I grab a belaying pin off the rail.

You cur!

Swing an' lunge, duck an' dodge! Black Dog's fat face in my sights! I'm going to smash his teeth in! But suddenly, my head explodes— betrayed from behind, a laceration to the cranium— an' down I go.

Wake up, back in the hold, this time, with a *leg iron* 'round my ankle. So I never see us make our way past Weston an' Watchet, Foreland Point, Ilfracombe an' Bull Point, out into the grey Atlantic.

Some lackey brings me food an' drink... Roger. Roger's the lackey.

"I saw your predicament," he says, "so I joined up. Volunteered."

But there's somethin' funny about Roger just now.

I grab him 'round the neck an' hold him down— Roger's not a big fella. Reach into his pocket an'... money.

MARINER (CONT'D): Just as I thought. "Getcha a pint," all innocent.

"I didn't know! I didn't know! Crimp said he just wanted to talk to you!"

Fuckin' Roger. Roger the Dodger. Roger, now my betrayer.

Outta me sight!

Seven days later they take the leg iron off. Far out to sea now.

Then I'm standing in Black Dog's cabin. All dark under the aftdeck.

So, Black Dog, where we goin'?

"South America," he says, "Yer specialty."

So there I am. On a privateer ship, not a *pirate* ship as Black Dog is quick to remind me, proud of his letter of marque, proud of his seal of approval from the king.

"You're part of a legitimate enterprise," he says. "Thievin' an' killin' for your king. For God an' country. Come back a rich man."

But the thing is, I don't wanna be part of this enterprise, legitimate or no. I want to be home with my boy, my pukin', sick, miserable boy.

It's unbelievable. You go out for a drink— *one drink!*— shut up— an' look what happens.

SCENE 4

MARINER: The Sun comes up upon the left,
  Out of the sea comes he!
  An' he shines bright, an' on the right
  Goes down into the sea.

We're goin' south.... Days go by.

Two hundred men crammed into a wooden sardine tin of a ship. Shoulder to shoulder. Above deck, below deck. Everywhere you go.

Men overhauling rigging,
Coiling an' oiling rope,
Changin', mendin', backin', reefin', balancin', loosenin', furlin' the sails,
cleanin' the guns,
checkin' the ballast,
stonin' an' swabbin' the deck,
an' the ever-present watch.
Day after day. Week after week.

Nothin' but the sun, an' the stars, an' the ship, an' the sea, an' the men, an' the never-ending work.

Two hundred men... ne'er-do-wells. Some lookin' for money.
Others trapped between the Devil an' the deep blue sea.
There's Simon, wants to impress his Dad.
An' James runnin' from the law.
An' John, runnin' from his wife.

For weeks, that's my life. A monotony broken only by crossin' the line.

A ritual that *has* to be performed, crossin' the line. See, what we call the pollywogs, that's any man who hasn't crossed the equator before, they're given a choice: pay a fine or get dunked in the drink. Most choose dunkin' in the drink. Goes like this: tie a line 'round your middle, just so.

(demonstrates)

They hoist you up the mast, but out, far away from the ship at the end of a yardarm. Nothin' but the rope holdin' you up, see. Hundred feet in the air. Dangle you there for a while. Arms an' legs flailin' 'round. Pissin' yourself.

An' then you drop. Fall fall fall an' fall, till you hit the water, then down down down to the keel of the ship, an' then... up again to the top of the yardarm.

This three times over

Fall, splash, down, 'n up!

Fall, splash, down, 'n up!

MARINER (CONT'D): Fall, splash, down, 'n up!

Don't worry, almost nobody dies.

An' that's nothin.' I was on a destroyer in World War II, there the pollywogs had like these electrified rods jabbed into their pobbly-wobblies. The "Devil's Tongue" they called it. Couldn't do it today, now could ya? Bloody heroes are all gone.

I tell 'em to initiate Roger, the look of him, ya know, the look of a novice, the look of a little fella in need of initiatin.' Now Roger, he insists he's crossed the line before, which he has, but they don't care. An' I enjoy every minute of it. Fall, splash, down, 'n up.

Fall, splash, down, 'n up.

An' Roger... squealin' like a butchered pig. I reckon we're almost even now.

An' we sail off, into the southern seas.

SCENE 5

MARINER: You know you're getting close to South America 'cuz the air smells sweet, you can see birds, an' the water changes color. First piss yellow, then blood red with these great big batches of shrimp.

Sail on. Get close to land. Swampy islands off the coast of Brazil.

An' that's where they need me: guide us 'round the shoals an' dangerous shores. Hiding out we are. Like a snake waitin' for its prey.

Then we see her on the horizon: a Spanish galleon comin' up the coast. Just what we've been waiting for. She sees us, turns tail an' tries to get away. But Spanish galleons, they might be big, but they are *slow*... An' away we go!

Men race to their posts. Powder monkeys bring gunpowder up from below. Ports open, cannons roll out, fires lighted, sails trimmed, ready for battle!

But wait, she's faster than we thought. She keeps headin' south down the coast an' we followin' behind.

A day. A week. On an' on we chase this Spanish galleon south, *way bloody south!* Further south than we ever intended to go. An' she's just a toy ship on the horizon, always out of reach.

Weather turns cold. But we keep going. Black Dog's orders. An' you can't argue with your captain. So, we're gonna catch that bloody galleon. An' then sure enough, little by little, we start to gain on her. 'Til we can make out her colors, an' her sides.

Then a fog rolls in. An' the wind shifts.

Big as she is, she's forced to tack to starboard, but we can hold tight to the wind... an' we've got her. We start sliding past her stern. Our broadside against her backside. Our twelve starboard guns against the single cannon she's got mounted on her stern. Rest of her guns pointin' at nothin.'

Wait for Black Dog's order... Wait...

"Fire!" An' all hell breaks loose. Hundredweight of deadly lead unleashes on the galleon!

Fire up her arse!

The cannons fire an' recoil! Fire an' recoil!

Round after round into the galleon's stern, we smash her rudder, take out her mizzen an' blast her officer's deck to kingdom come!

An' then hard to starboard! An' we swing 'round an' come back across her bow. She gets more of her guns on us this time, tries to take our rigging out. But it's nothing compared to what we're doin' to her.

MARINER (CONT'D): Then we're right alongside, firin' guns an' cannons point blank! BOOM! BOOM! BOOM! Smoke an' shrapnel fill the air! BOOM! BOOM! BOOM! The crunch of ship on ship, an' still we fire! BOOM! BOOM! BOOM! An' then the crew leaps over the bulwarks an' take control of the ship! Aaaaahhhhhhhh!

It's fuckin' *awesome!*

Smoke clears an' we go to round up the crew.

But, strange, we can only find one man. We look high an' low, but that's it... the ship's empty. Totally an' completely empty. It doesn't make sense. They couldn't have abandoned ship... Hundreds of miles from shore... water freezing.

Damndest thing I ever seen.

Anyhow, this one fella's in bad shape. Yellin', screamin', crazed. Can't tell what he's sayin' 'cuz he's speakin' Spanish or somethin.'

Something weird going on here an' this fellow all that's left for us to work our spleen on. So Black Dog tells us to gather all the roaches, maggots, an' rats on the ship an' put 'em in a barrel. No crew maybe, but there's plenty of vermin.

Black Dog takes his knife, slashes the man's arms, stomach, an' face. Big open wounds. Then, Black Dog opens his mouth, teeth like a canine, bites down on the man's shoulder. The man howls. Black Dog spits chunks of flesh an' blood on the deck.

An' then we take the man an' we force him into the barrel... barrel full of all the roaches, maggots, an' rats, squirmin' 'round on top of each other, tryin' to get out... we force the man into the barrel an' hammer on the lid.

Then we set the Flying Dutchman, or whatever the fuck she is, ablaze an' sail off. Fire rises high an' bright. We can hear him screamin' as she slips into the fog.
            (pause)
An' the prize? 30,000 gold moidores – coins – worth about 40,000 pound. After Black Dog's take an' the Crown's take, that still leaves 160 pounds per man. An' I get a double share! In your dollars... that's over 100,000. Biggest payday 'a me life.

SCENE 6

MARINER: An' then, home! To me boy— dead or alive. But see that ship, with only a single man as her crew, she did damage to us. Split rigging. Ripped sails. Holes in the hull.

Black Dog, he says to me, "We need repairs. Find me a haven, navigator."

So I chart a course to the nearest land. Further south to the Falkland Islands...

A few rocks in the south Atlantic whose chief inhabitants are *penguins*.

An' we anchor off shore an' repair our ship.

A few days in, an' Black Dog announces he wants some penguins. *Penguins!*

What you want penguins for? I ask him.

Turns out, Black Dog's been collecting animals from all over the world in honor of the King... King George the First, who signs off on his letters of marque an' thus legitimizes an illegitimate business. Building a zoo he is. His own fuckin' Noah's Arc in honor of the King.

Black Dog says he's already got toucans, an' jaguars, an' lions, an' tropical snakes, an' now for what'll be the prized item... penguins.

But how we gonna get them back? I ask him. They'll be deader than dead by the time we get back to England.

"Exactly," he says, "an' that's why we need hundreds of penguins. So by the time we get back, one or two might still be alive."

Ah, come on Black Dog, let's just go home. Forget the penguins.

Black Dog pulls out a knife, puts it to me throat, grabs me head an' pulls it back!

"What'd you say?"

I said, let's get some penguins.

So we go ashore, start grabbin' penguins an' tossing 'em in sacks, laughin' havin' a grand ol' time. The penguins've never seen people before, so they're not scared. Just stand there looking dumb.

He enthusiastically embodies the memory.

An' we grab an' toss, grab an' toss, grab an' toss!

Roger at my side. "This is fun!"

Yeah, Roger, this is fun.

He stops suddenly.

MARINER (CONT'D): Then we see— a warrah. Yeah, a bloody warrah walking along big as life.

What's a warrah, you ask? Yeah, you would. Like a cross between a fox an' a wolf. Gone they are. Killed off by shepherds who settled the island. Eighteen seventy-six, the last one died in a zoo in London. They call it, human caused extension. Curious they are— an' this one's no different.

Come to investigate the abduction of the penguins.

Black Dog takes a bit of fish meat, puts it on a stick, holds it out. Warrah comes closer... coming closer... "come to papa..." Then we grab 'im an' toss 'im in a cage!

Spend a couple more days roughing up the place. We take our bounty— 137 squawkin', flappin', shittin' penguins in wooden crates— an' stow 'em in the hold. Black Dog takes the warrah to his cabin like it's some kind 'a pet.

Then we sail away from the Falklands. Homeward bound! Stomachs an' pockets full!

> *(to the spirits)*

An' were you watchin' when we sailed away, when we set fire to the galleon, when we raped the island? Were ya? Were ya?

> *(pause)*

They never answer.

But I'll tell ya' this, the sky an' sea go all black. Storm clouds movin' in fast. No time to lower the sails. We have to turn the ship with the wind, get ready to ride her out. Speed increasing.

Swells under the stern. An' then POW!

An' now the storm-blast came, an' he
Was tyrannous an' strong:
He struck with his o'ertaking wings,
An' chased us south along.
With sloping mast an' dipping prow
As he who bends his head,
The ship drove fast, loud roared the blast,
An' southward aye we fled.

Sea crackling! Wind pounding! A massive wave in front of the ship... growing, building, swelling like the engorging belly of a beast! We ride to the top! An' then shoot down his back! The bow digs deep into the next! Water slams across the deck!

Cut the lines! *Cut the lines!* Cut 'em! *CUT 'EM!* GO GO GO!

The MARINER physically embodies the following as if reliving it.

MARINER (CONT'D): Another wave across the deck. Roger! I run— stumble, fall, crawl— look over the side.

He's tied his leg to the mast with a rope— smart lad, Roger. But now he's hanging over the side of the ship, waves slamming him against the hull. I pull on the rope. I pull Roger up. He vomits water across the deck.

But no time to recover 'cuz the ship lists to starboard! Further an' further!

HOLD ON!

She leans till the yardarms kiss the sea! We're going over for sure! But then she rolls back an' we tumble across deck!

An' then... I see the strangest sight: the warrah. Wandering around on the deck. Like he's askin,' "What's all the racket 'bout, boys?"

Curious fucks, didn't I tell ya? Well, curiosity killed the cat, or, in this case, the warrah 'cuz at that moment a line snaps, whips across the deck an' cuts the warrah in two! One half over here, the other half over there. Black Dog sees it, he shouts, "Monty!"

He named the fucker. Named the warrah, *Monty*?!

But then a wave washes across the deck an' sweeps ol' Monty to a watery grave.

The storm rages all night.

An' we, we cling to the bowels of the ship like rats.

SCENE 7

MARINER: The next morning... silence. The sea. Calm, grey. Smooth as glass.

An' now there comes mist an' snow,
An' it grows wondrous cold.
An' ice, huge chunks of ice, *mast-high*, emerald green, come floating by.

An' through the drifts the snowy cliffs
Send a dismal sheen.

Ice here. Ice there. Ice all around.
It cracks an' growls, an' roars an' howls.
A dizzy, swooning sound.

Black Dog at my elbow.

"So, navigator, where are we?"

South, I tell 'im. Off the map. On the bottom of the goddamn world.

"Impossible!"

Well, look 'round!

Black Dog barkin' out orders now: "Extend the sails! Turn the ship 'round!
Due north! North, north!"

But when we trim what remains of our storm-beaten sails, the ship says, "I
think not" an' keeps going south, as if pulled by an invisible force.

An' the snow.

Huge bloody flakes. Fallin' on the prow, on the stern, on the rail an' the deck,
on the yardarms an' cross spars. Piling thick an' high, high an' thick. Giant
icicles forming under the lines.

Boys from Watney an' Plymouth not used to the freezing cold of this place.

See, you gotta imagine... you're on a wooden ship... no engine, no electricity,
no nothin.' You're workin' the foresail, tryin' to tease a little bit of life outa
the still, freezing air. At it for hours, an' you hardly notice the deadly cold
that's easing its way into your feet.

Till at last your watch ends, an' you can head below, for a cup of rum. Feels
good.

But not your feet... they're chunks of ice. Take off your boot have a look...
black frostbitten toes.

MARINER (CONT'D): Now, if you're lucky, a toe or two will shrivel up like a mummy's dick an' fall off. But if you're not, gangrene sets in an' your foot swells up... a pus-filled balloon. Then ya got two choices: saw your foot off— nothing but rum an' a bit a leather between your teeth— *or* the fire burns your whole body up an' you die in agony.

That's what happens to the first mate, William. Only a few hours between first chill an' burning alive. Lucky sod.

An' the ice just keeps getting' thicker. I'm navigatin' through narrow channels an' fjords, green cliffs on either side. Totally lost. 'Till at last there's nowhere left to take the ship that won't crush her sides into matchsticks. We're just sittin' there. Ice-coated ship in a land of mist an' snow... End of the line.

SCENE 8

MARINER: An' then... an Albatross.

Glides in, spirit-like, out of the fog. Wings twelve feet wide. Descends down. Lands, stands, commands the bow rail.

"You think he's hungry?" says Roger. Like I said, bleedin' heart.

Still, I go down below to our meager stores. Get a bit of moldy biscuit an' come back up an' feed it to him— 'til 'round an' 'round he flies again.

An' then, with a loud crack, the ice parts.

The cliffs move back an' a narrow gap opens before us. The mist still hangs low an' thick, can't see more than fifty feet, but a light breeze kicks up from the south, an' slowly, surely, we begin to move out of our icy prison.

An' the Albatross following.

"Must be good luck," says Roger.

Well, what do we know about this Albatross?

Quite a lot, it turns out. Family Diomedeidae, order Procellariiformes, class Aves, phylum Chordata, kingdom Animalia.

The family name Diomedeidae refers, of course, to the Greek myth, the one 'bout the companions of Diomedes who got turned into birds. You know the one. Yeah?

> *He realizes we don't know the myth he is referring to.*

No. Well, try Wikipedia when you get home.

The order Procelariiformes means, "shaped for the storm." The albatross is a sailor of the winds. Can stay aloft for five years.

He mates for life. Finds a partner an' they create a dance that's unique to the two of 'em alone. An' when it ends, they never dance again.

An' if that's not a metaphor for marriage, I don't know what is.

Albatross doesn't age. I'm not sayin' he's immortal, or anything like that, but, see, physically, he's the same at sixty as he is at ten. He doesn't decline into dotage, with cloudy eye an' creaking wing. No, he sails the world, 'round an' 'round in fantastic circles.... But not *this* albatross....

In mist or cloud, on mast or shroud,

He perched for vespers nine.

He just sits there.

MARINER (CONT'D): Days go by an' he becomes like... a little part 'a me. Friends in a friendless place. Out here in this cold, dark sea an' two living creatures are drawn to each other for reasons unknown.

I feed him, talk to him, I even sing to him.

Sings: "Down Among the Dead Men"

Here's a health to the king and a lasting peace,
May faction end and wealth increase.
Come let us drink it while we have breath,
For there's no drinkin' after death.
And he who would this health deny
Down among the dead men, down among the dead men,
Down, Down, Down, Down,
Down among the dead men let him lie.

Guess it was a kind of dance.

I'm off-duty. I'm sittin' on deck, takin' target practice with my crossbow.
     (gesturing shooting his crossbow)
Albatross is sitting there, too.

He looks at me. I look at him. An' then...

Gesture of shooting the albatross. Pause.

Yeah, I shoot the albatross. Hear the arrow enter his body with a *thunk*!

Massive bird drops down on the deck. Another thunk. Flutters an' flops.

I get up, walk over to him. Still flopping 'round. Reach down. Pull the arrow out. An' then I put the heel of my boot on his head an' push down. Push down hard. Not a thunk this time. More like a bunch 'a little cracks, as his skull an' beak give way under the pressure of my boot.

Was it like killing Christ? Was it like thunder an' lightening smote me all to hell?

Was it like that? ... No. It wasn't like that 'cuz nothing happened.

Though maybe, *maybe* I saw a misty white puff, a little flicker of light, as his soul rose from his body an' ascended to the heavens. Maybe I saw that... or maybe I didn't. I don't know.

But I *do* know what you're thinking.

Why? Why'd you do it? Your last chance to save yourself, befriend this bird an' feed your soul on the fruit of heaven, an' you cut off your own hand? Why would you do that?

MARINER (CONT'D): You're dying to know, right? 'Cause this is the moment. The crux. The act that separates my past from my eternal present. Probably the only thing you actually know 'bout this story, right. Well, that an' the "water, water everywhere" bit, which, don't worry, is comin' up.

Harmless ol' bird. Pickin' at scraps. Makin' the sailors' burden less burdensome. "What the fuck is wrong with me?" you ask. What black mold in some dark corner of your soul made you butcher that ageless sailor of the wind?

You must know, right? To make sense of it all? To provide you with a reasonable psychological explanation to satisfy your Post-Freudian concept of human nature!!!!

"WHY? WHY? TELL ME WHY?"

Sometimes there is no why...

SCENE 9

MARINER: The sun now rises on the right:
  Out of the sea comes he,
  Still hid in mist, an' on the left
  Goes down into the sea...

We're goin' north.

Black Dog gets in me face.

"What's wrong with ya?! You killed the bird who made the breeze to blow!"

Raises his fist like he's gonna hit me. He stops. See something in my eyes. Afraid 'a me he is. Roger looks on. He's afraid, too.

Yeah, I killed the bird. What of it?

Two hundred men look on me with fear. Oh, they'd kill me if they dared.

An' then... *then...* the fog an' mist lift!

I mean they rise up an' blow away. An' the sun! The warm sun... blue sky, blue ocean!

It's a miracle!

Now, everyone says I killed the bird who brought the fog an' mist! Fair weather friends right? 'Tis right, they say, such birds to slay who bring fog an' mist.

Black Dog gives me a hug. Roger, my mate again. Two hundred men all my best friends. The crew take the carcass of the albatross an' hang it high on the mast. Our good luck charm.

The fair breeze blew, the white foam flew,
  The furrows followed free;
  We were the first that ever burst
  Into that silent sea.

In those days, sailing into the South Pacific was like jumping off into eternity. The far side of the world. Ripe with possibility.

SCENE 10

MARINER: An' all the while, you, Spirit, were scuddin' along nine fathom deep, stalkin' us like a cat stalks a mouse. Watchin', waitin', toyin' with us. Till we were far out into the deep blue sea, a thousand miles from any shore... an' then:

Down dropt the breeze, the sails dropt down,
'Twas sad as sad could be;
And we did speak only to break
The silence of the sea!

All in a hot and copper sky,
The bloody Sun, at noon,
Right up above the mast did stand,
No bigger than the Moon.

Day after day, day after day,
We stuck, nor breath nor motion;
As idle as a painted ship
Upon a painted ocean.

Water, water, everywhere,
And all the boards did shrink;
Water, water everywhere,
Nor any drop to drink.

There. Ya heard it. Ya happy now? Feelin' smart?

But look. We're dyin' 'a thirst alright, but Coleridge doesn't get how it works. We don't drink water on the ship! Ever! It becomes a cesspool in three weeks.

No, we drink *rum*. Pint a day. Neat. *Your* livers couldn't handle it. An' now we're down to a tablespoon 'a rum a day.

An' the sun just keeps blazin'. Men take their clothes off. Bury themselves under the slack sails, under ropes, under empty barrels.

Then we run out of food. Except for one thing. No, no, no! We do have *one* thing. Penguins. Well, the eleven survivors. So we attack. Snap their necks, tear their feathers from their flesh. Warm sloppy meat. Makes you gag, but keeps you alive.

An' then... Oh, God no!... The rum runs out!

MARINER (CONT'D): Let me tell you 'bout dyin' a' thirst. First, you get dizzy, your head is poundin'. Nothin' I can't handle you think. Then the cramps set in. Legs ache. Get clumsy, stumble, an' fall. You get fever, nausea. Then you can't breathe. See, the fluid in your lungs brings oxygen to your blood. As you dry up, gets harder to breathe. An' every time you blink, your eyelids stick shut like they're sewn together. Opening your eyes is like ripping the stitches out.

At some point it dawns on you there's only one thing you can do: drink your own piss.

The first piss is yellow. Pure. Lemonade stand piss. Grateful, you drink it down. Next time, it's darker, saltier. Third cup is orange. Smells bad, but you drink it anyway. Then brown. An' then black. Like coffee. Only it smells like rottin' meat. No, ya' can't drink that piss. An' then ya stop pissin' all together.

I look up, I see the crew surrounding me like a pack of rabid dogs. All skin an' bones an' burning eyes.

"All this is punishment," Black Dog says, "for you shootin' that bird."

Uh, ya think? Bloody genius.

Black Dog orders the albatross pulled down from the mast, threads a rope under his wings, ties the rope off, hangs the massive dead bird 'round my neck.

"Wear this to remind you of what you've done. Take it off an' I'll kill ya."

The MARINER feels the weight of the bird around his neck.

Thirty pounds the bird is. Like carrying a dead child. Only worse: wing-tips draggin' at my feet... head nothing but grey pulp an' broken beak... an' a stench to make you heave your guts.

Then passed a weary time. Each throat
Was parched, and glazed each eye.

Then looking westward, I beheld
A something in the sky.

At first it seemed a little speck,
And then it seemed a mist;
It moved and moved, and took at last
A certain shape, I wist.

With throats unslaked, with black lips baked,
We could not laugh nor wail;
Through utter drought all dumb we stood!
I bit my arm, I sucked the blood,
And cried, A sail! A sail!

MARINER (CONT'D): We're saved!
See! See!
How fast she moves!
We're saved! We're saved!
> (beat)

But wait. The ship... it's shape an' lines... a burnt out skeleton.

Good Christ! It's the Spanish galleon! The one we set ablaze so many weeks ago.

An' as she nears, we see a grizzly pair... Death an' the Maiden. With bony hand he steers the ship, an' she, naked, cleaves herself to him in ghastly copulation.

Her lips are red, her looks are free,
Her locks are yellow as gold,
Her skin is as white as leprosy,
The Nightmare Life-in-Death is she,
Who thicks man's blood with cold.

The burnt-out hulk alongside comes.

An' now they're tossing dice.

The Maiden cries, "The game is done. I've won! I've won!" An' then she whistles thrice.
> (A whistle)

The stars rush out, Death rises up. On long dark wings, he hovers above our ship.

Then one by one, the star-crossed crew,
Too quick for groan or sigh,
Each turned his face with a ghastly pang,
An' cursed me with his eye.

Four times fifty living men
Without a sigh or groan,
A heavy thump, a lifeless lump,
Each falls down one by one.

An' now I see their souls rise from their bodies. Four times fifty misty, white puffs – *this time* for certain – rise up an' pass me by.

SCENE 11

MARINER (CONT'D): Daybreak an' I'm alone.

An' I know what the dice game was about. Death won my shipmates, an' the Maiden, Life-in-Death, she won me.

Alone, alone, all, all alone,
Alone on a wide, wide sea.

My only companions the rotting corpses of the crew.

I do not eat. I do not drink an' still I do not die.

What'd I do? *I killed a bird!* Was it so bad!?

Someone drinks a bottle of water. Throws the cap away. Later the cap gets loaded on a barge an' falls into the sea. Bounces along on the waves, eddies 'round a gigantic continent of trash that's floating in the South Pacific, breaks off, washes up on the shore of a little island, where thousands of albatross make their nests. A mother bird sees the bright blue cap an' thinks it's food... a lovely berry full of goodness. Tenderly she feeds it to her growing chick... a baby. An' the baby dies, its gut jammed with bits of plastic *someone* fuckin' threw away without a thought.

Am I the only one guilty of sin?

I crawl out onto the bowsprit, albatross still hanging 'round my neck, hoping to drop an' sink to the bottom of the ocean an' be free.

But when I look down, the sea has become a hive of roiling snakes... red, green, blue, yellow, large an' small, as far as the eye can see... horrifying, slimy creatures all!

I truly am in hell!

All I can do is watch the hellish serpents wriggle an' squirm.

An' as I do... I see their eyes... their tails... their scales... are actually kind of... wonderful...

An' every track they leave a flash of golden fire...

An' the way they move... driven by a unquenchable desire for life...

How beautiful are all living things!

An' I take the bird... the albatross 'round my neck... an' I cradle him in my arms.

An' in his mangled face, I see the wounded face of my boy.

My child. A little part of me he is. My son.

MARINER (CONT'D): An' I pray. I pray. Without words, without thought, I pray for the bird, for the snakes, for the Crimp, for the Spanish Sailor, for Black Dog, for the crew. For James an' Peter an' Matthias an' John an' Will an' Thaddeus an' Tom an' Robert an' Henry an' Evan an' Luke an' Zachary an' David an' Marcus an' Richard an' Daniel an' Gareth an' Christopher an' Oliver an' Tobias an' Jeremy an' Koto an' Manuel an' Franz an' François an' Liam an' Devon an' Georg an' Assam an' Samuel an' Jack an' Edward an' Cole an' Simeon an' Charlie an' Jacob an' Louis an' Joshua an' Noah an' Ben an' Chen an' Theodore an' Joseph, an' Roger. An' my son. For all of them, I pray.

An' the rope dissolves from 'round my neck, an' the albatross slips off, slips between my arms, down into the sea...

SCENE 12

MARINER (CONT'D): I sleep for days. Months. I don't know.

I dream it rains.
My lips are wet, my throat is cold,
My garments all are dank;
Sure I had drunken in my dreams,
An' still my body drank.

I moved, an' could not feel my limbs:
I was so light— almost
I thought that I had died in sleep,
An' was a blessed ghost.

I dream that the dead men rise up. Two hundred dead men on their feet working the ship. Black Dog at the wheel. Roger on the shroud. An' the ship moves on, driven by a zombie crew.

At the keel nine fathom deep, the Spirit who slid from the land of mist an' snow, it was he who made the ship to go.

An' I open my eyes. An' the ship is standing in Bristol Harbor.

The harbour-bay was clear as glass,
So smoothly it was strewn!
An' on the bay the moonlight lay,
An' the shadow of the moon.

An' the dead men, each one lays down flat. An' the ghostly image of the man, all light, a seraph-man, on every corpse there stands. Each man waves his hand... in blessing, farewell, or perhaps warning.

A massive roar as the waters part! The ship spins, a whirlpool sucks it down! Swallowed in one giant gulp by the sea! I should go down with it, down into the dark. But life surges within me an' I fight against the maelstrom!

HELP!

I go under!

HELP!

I go under again!

HELP!!!!

> *MARINER struggles and then stops.*

An' then... I'm on land. Firm as firm can be! HOME!

An'... Hermit. Hermit standing there, singin' his hymns.

MARINER (CONT'D): He backs away from me, crosses his brow, sayin', "What manner of man art thou?"

I open my mouth, give him an answer...

An' as I do, for the first time my body is wracked with the woeful agony, my head is aflame, my heart is unbound, an' from my mouth an explosion, a puss-filled boil, bursting up from my bowels, an explosion of words...

THERE WAS A SHIP! A RUINED HOUSE, SHACK MORE LIKE. FIRE AN' RECOIL! FIRE AN' RECOIL! BOOM BOOM! AN ALBATROSS. LANDS, STANDS, FOR VESPERS NINE. THUNK! THE FAIR BREEZE BLEW, THE WHITE FOAM FLEW, THE FURROWS FOLLOWED FREE! WATER WATER EVERYWHERE NOR ANY DROP TO DRINK! A SPECK, A MIST, A SHAPE, I WIST! THE WATER SERPENTS COILED AN' SWAM! A SERAPH-MAN, ON EVERY CORPSE THERE STANDS! HELP! HELP...!

An' when I finish my story... I'm free...
>
> *(stops, a breath)*

The Hermit says: "With your cruel bow you laid full low the harmless Albatross."

I did, I say.

An' he says: "The spirit who lived in the land of mist and snow, he loved the bird who loved the man who shot him with his bow."

I know that. Now.

An' the hermit, went like one who hath been stunned, a sadder an' wiser man.

I walk back home.

See the neighborhood whore, sittin' on the stoop across the lane, head down.

But my house is gone. Burned out. Nothin' but blackened ash an' timber. A black hole of charred remains.

Whore raises her head.

"So yer back," she says. "You missed the fun."

What fun, says I?

"Bed of straw... fire from the hearth, mum drunk as hell, an', well, you can see the rest. Ya should've stayed. Leavin' him with the like a her. *Ya should've fuckin' stayed!*"

Then I walk down the lane without looking back. Been walking ever since. An' the spirits beside me.

MARINER (CONT'D): At uncertain hours, the agony returns. An' till my ghastly tale is told, my heart within me burns.

I pass like night from land to land. The moment his face I see, I know the man who must hear me. To him my tale I teach.

Farewell. But this I tell
To thee, the final piece:
He prayeth well, who loveth well
Both man and bird and beast.

He prayeth best, who loveth best
All things great and small;
For the dear God who loveth us,
He made and loveth all.

Lights down.

END OF PLAY

ABOUT STAGE RIGHTS

Based in Los Angeles and founded in 2000, Stage Rights is one of the foremost independent theatrical publishers in the United States, providing stage performance rights for a wide range of plays and musicals to theater companies, schools, and other producing organizations across the country and internationally. As a licensing agent, Stage Rights is committed to providing each producer the tools they need for financial and artistic success. Stage Rights is dedicated to the future of live theatre, offering special programs that champion new theatrical works.

To view all of our current plays and musicals, visit:

www.stagerights.com